Thank You For A Great Year!

To my teacher,

Thank you for a great year!

Signed,

_____

Year _____

This is your name
in my neatest writing:

_____

This is what your
autograph should look
like when you become
famous:

My favorite outfit that you wear is

_____

_____

_____

Here is a picture of you in it:

Here is my best portrait of you

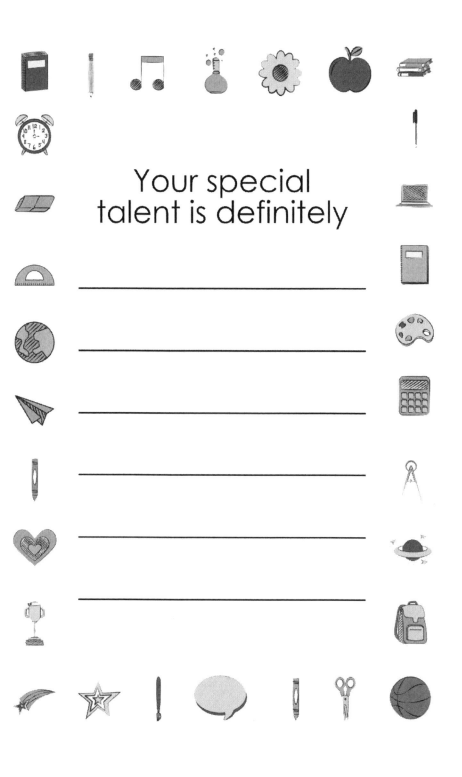

Your special
talent is definitely

_____

_____

_____

_____

_____

_____

I really liked our
field trip to

_____

_____

because

_____

_____

_____

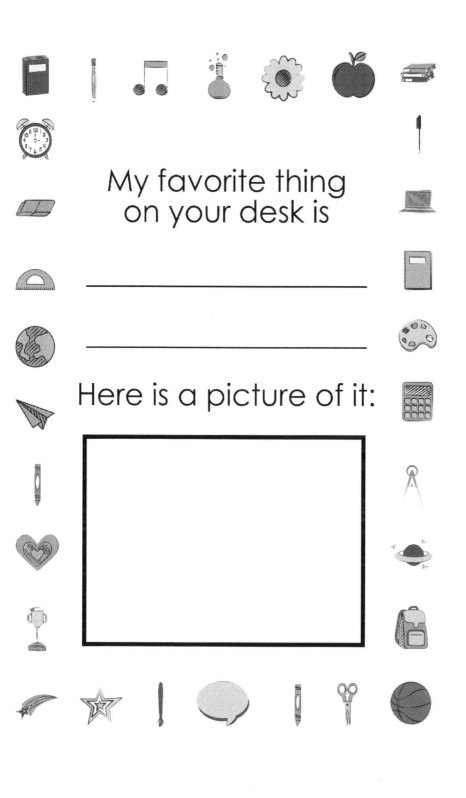

My favorite thing on your desk is

_____

_____

Here is a picture of it:

My favorite joke you like to tell is

Remember when

_____

_____

_____

_____

_____

_____

My favorite poster
in the room is

_____

_____

_____

_____

_____

_____

Here is a portrait
of our principal

My favorite part about math was

_____

_____

_____

_____

_____

_____

My favorite part about social studies was

_____

_____

_____

_____

_____

_____

My favorite part about science was

_____

_____

_____

_____

_____

_____

My favorite part about reading was

_____

_____

_____

_____

_____

_____

My favorite part about writing was

_____

_____

_____

_____

_____

_____

My favorite project
we worked on was

_____

_____

_____

_____

_____

_____

My favorite book
in your room is

_____

_____

_____

_____

_____

_____

Remember when

_____

_____

_____

_____

_____

_____

My favorite classroom guest was

_____

_____

_____

_____

_____

_____

I was surprised in your classroom when

I was a little sad in
your classroom when

_____

_____

_____

_____

_____

_____

I got a little scared
in your classroom
when

_____

_____

_____

_____

_____

_____

I was so happy in your classroom when

_____

_____

_____

_____

_____

_____

Map of your classroom

(In case you are ever lost!)

Remember when

_____

_____

_____

_____

_____

_____

You made me laugh when

_____

_____

_____

_____

_____

_____

You really helped
me when

_____

_____

_____

_____

_____

_____

My favorite advice you gave was

_____

_____

_____

_____

_____

_____

You made me feel special when

_____

_____

_____

_____

_____

_____

You are a role model because

What I will miss most about your classroom is

_____

_____

_____

_____

_____

_____

What I will miss most about you is

A picture of me so
you won't forget!